NANUET PUBLIC LIBRARY

2 2624 00936 9302

D1037011

Brigid's Cloak

AN ANCIENT IRISH STORY

For Brigid Aileen Milligan, now an author herself,
who waited many years for this book, with all my love.
— *B. M.*

For Jane Knowles, with much love.
— *H. C.*

Text © 2002 by Bryce Milligan
Illustrations © 2002 by Helen Cann
Published 2002 by Eerdmans Books for Young Readers
An imprint of Wm. B. Eerdmans Publishing Company
255 Jefferson S.E., Grand Rapids, Michigan 49503
P.O. Box 163, Cambridge CB3 9PU U.K.

All rights reserved
Printed and bound in Hong Kong

02 03 04 05 06 07   7 6 5 4 3 2 1

ISBN 0-8028-5224-6

A catalog record of this book is available from the Library of Congress.

The illustrations were created in mixed media.
The display type was set in Fraktur.
The text type was set in Venetian.

Brigid's Cloak

An Ancient Irish Story

NANUET
PUBLIC
LIBRARY

Written by BRYCE MILLIGAN

Illustrated by HELEN CANN

EERDMANS BOOKS FOR YOUNG READERS

Grand Rapids, Michigan ❖ Cambridge, U.K.

a wild and windy night it was, fifteen centuries ago, that a very special child was born in Ireland. The baby's father was Duffy, a warrior prince and the lord of Faughart Hill. But the child's mother was not a princess at all. Far from it. Little Brigid — for that was the baby's name — was born in a cold hut outside the walls of Duffy's hill fort, a slave child among slave women.

The wind groaned and swirled that night, and likely it seemed to tear the thatch from the roof. But when the baby gave her first cry, the wind shushed to a whisper. Then all over the hill the people came out and looked to the sky, swept clean and cloudless.

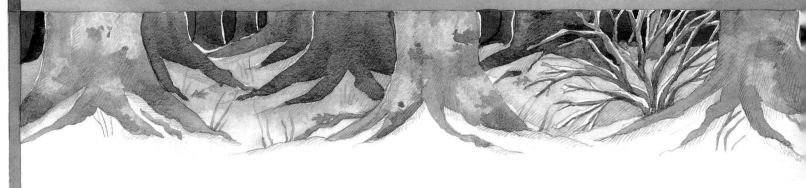

"Listen," they said to each other in wonder. "The stars are singing." And it's singing they were, not a song like you or I might sing, but a gathering of sweet crystal notes like birdsong and brook laughter in the spring.

The forest all around was so dense and dark that it was hard to tell where the trees ended and the sky began. Then someone said, "Look, a star has fallen into the forest!"

But it wasn't a star at all. It was a tiny lantern that twinkled as it swung back and forth from the top of a tall staff. A very old man appeared at the edge of the forest, and it was he who carried the star-lantern. He had holly leaves in his long white hair, and he wore long flowing robes. The people backed away as he came up the hill. They knew what he was. He was a Druid — one of the powerful wizards who lived alone in the oak grove in the center of the great forest.

He came directly to the door of the hut where the newborn child lay cradled in her mother's arms.

Now the women in the hut were all Christians, but Druids were not. Druids worshipped the moon and the tree spirits, and they talked to the fairy folk who lived beneath the hills. And everyone knew that Druids could tell the future.

"God be with you," said the young mother politely.

"It's with me your God has been," he replied in a voice wise and fierce and full of truth. "I was told in a dream to bring this gift to the child born on the night of the singing stars."

The old Druid held out a beautiful blue cloak. Now in those days blue was a rare color for any sort of cloth, and the women were surprised. Blue was a royal color. The old Druid wrapped the baby in the cloak and then held her up high in the air and said, "This cloak will be a sign of your God's favor. I am one of the fathers of old Ireland. I greet little Brigid, who will be a mother to the new Ireland that is to come."

Now these were strange words indeed, and not soon forgotten, but no one knew what they meant. And the Druid didn't explain either. He simply placed Brigid carefully in her mother's arms, made a magic sign of blessing with his staff, and strode away into the dark.

ell and ill, ten years went by. Brigid was in charge of a small flock of Prince Duffy's sheep. One bitterly cold December evening, Brigid was bringing her flock home, as she did every night. The little shepherdess pulled her old blue cloak close about her shoulders. The Druid's gift was now little more than a worn and tattered cloth, yet it was her most treasured possession. Brigid wore it every day and often wondered about the meaning of the Druid's words — for her mother and many another had repeated them to her over and over.

The first stars were beginning to twinkle. Brigid loved this time of day so close to Christmas, for she would pretend that the brightest star in the east was the Christmas star. She liked to imagine that she was one of those shepherds so long ago, making her way to a stable in Bethlehem to see the baby Jesus.

In her own stable, Brigid shut up the sheep for the night, and patted each of the cows as she called them by name. When all were settled in their stalls and fresh hay had been spread, Brigid knelt down as she always did to say a prayer of thanks. There were no wolves today, and all her animals were safe.

NANUET PUBLIC LIBRARY
149 Church Street
Nanuet, New York 10954

hen Brigid stood to go in for supper, she rubbed her eyes
in disbelief. She was no longer in her own familiar stable.
She was in a stable, true enough, but outside there were no forest
sounds, and the air was dry, warm, and dusty. Up the hill from the
stable, she saw a village of curious flat-roofed houses and narrow
streets. But there was Duffy! Or was it? A man dressed in oddly
colored robes came striding down the hill.

   "What is taking you so long, daughter?" he demanded. "We
have many visitors, and they want their suppers."

Brigid followed him up the hill and into a small stone building. Duffy, it seemed, was an innkeeper in this strange place, and he soon had Brigid ladling out bowls of stew, cutting thick slices of hard bread, filling and refilling cups of wine. There were dishes to wash and rooms to clean and beds to make. She worked hard, long into the night.

At last, Brigid had a chance to rest. She sat down on a bench by the door, wondering where in the world this place might be, and why she was there.

Just then, there was a soft knocking at the door. "There's no more room!" Duffy shouted from another room. "Tell them to go away."

"Please," a man's voice outside said, "I must find a place for my wife to rest."

The voice was so kind and tired. Maybe, she thought, she could talk Duffy into finding just one more bed. Wearily, Brigid rose and opened the door. Outside, behind the man, a young woman sat on a very small donkey.

"Thank you," said the man. "My name is Joseph, and this is my wife, Mary."

Brigid felt as one does when a candle is lit in a very dark room. She now knew exactly where she was and what she had to do. "Come quickly," she said, leading them away from the inn and down the hill.

In the stable, she helped Joseph lay a bed of soft hay on the floor. They covered the hay with Joseph's cloak. Even though it did not seem cold to Brigid, Mary was shivering. Brigid took off her old cloak and put it around Mary's shoulders. "You will need some water," she said when they were settled, and she hurried back to the inn.

When she returned with a heavy clay jar of water, Brigid could hear from inside the stable the soft sounds of a newborn baby. Joseph gave the child to Brigid to hold, as he made Mary more comfortable. Lovingly she held the child, then carefully laid him in the cow's hay manger.

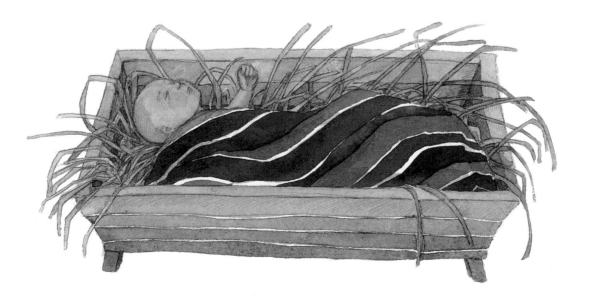

"Blessed are you among all women," she said to Mary, "and blessed is your holy child." Joseph and Mary smiled at her, and a comforting golden light seemed to grow around them. From the skies above came the sweetest music Brigid had ever heard, yet it sounded familiar. It was the music of brooks and bird song, of bells and harps, of oceans and lakes. For that one moment, the earth itself sang out in joy.

Brigid's awe was broken by the soft voice of Mary. "Thank you, child of the West," she said, then she handed Brigid's cloak to Joseph, who placed it around Brigid's shoulders.

"Your generosity will be remembered always," he added.

t hen there was the sound of steps and voices outside. "Where is that child?" a voice said. "Brigid!" called another. "Look! What is that light in the stable there?"

Brigid looked up as the door was thrust open. But there were no shepherds or wise kings at the door. Instead, it was her own mother and some of the other slave women from Faughart Hill. Snow swirled in the open door with a gust of cold night air. The holy family was gone, and Brigid felt the ache in her knees from kneeling too long. But the ache in her heart was much worse — she longed for the holy scene that had vanished so quickly. Instead here she was in her very own stable, surrounded by her own sheep and cows.

"What has taken you so long!" demanded her mother. "It's late and cold and we were worried." Then she stopped her scolding with a gasp. "What is this?" she said, pointing to her daughter's cloak.

All the women gathered around to examine the cloak, though none would touch it.

Brigid pulled the old blue cloth from her shoulders only to find it changed. It was a deep rich blue again, blue like the eastern sky at twilight, and on it were dozens of tiny glowing stars.

"I was in Bethlehem . . . ," she began.

Historical Note

Saint Brigid of Ireland

Brigid was born around the year 450 A.D., just a few years before St. Patrick died. She grew up to become one of Ireland's most beloved saints.

Saint Brigid's generosity and her cloak were long remembered in Ireland. Brigid founded many convents all over Ireland where the poor could always find shelter and a meal. Her cloak, which played a part in several miracles later in her life, became a sign of protection to the people of Ireland as well. A common blessing among friends was the hope that they would be *fa bhrat Bhrighde*, "under Brigid's cloak." A very old Scottish nursery rhyme mentions "Seynt Brigid and her brat, Seynt Colum and his cat." (The "brat" is the same as the Irish word "bhrat," and it means "cloak.") To this very day, the cathedral in Bruges, Belgium, keeps in reverence a large blue cloak which is said to be Saint Brigid's very own. Saint Brigid's feast day is celebrated on the first of February.